Pocket
Celtic Prayers

COMPILED BY
Martin Wallace

CHURCH HOUSE
PUBLISHING

Church House Publishing
Church House
Great Smith Street
London SW1P 3NZ
Tel: 020 7898 1451
Fax: 020 7898 1449

ISBN 0 7151 4044 2

Published 1999 by The National Society
and Church House Publishing

Printed in England by the University Printing House,
Cambridge

CONTENTS

DEDICATED TO
DIANA, CAROLINE AND MATTHEW

INTRODUCTION

If prayer is about meeting with the living God, it can never be static, dead, used. Prayer not only arises out of every place and generation, but also moves across geography and history. Celtic spirituality emerges from the mists of the so-called Dark Ages, not only speaking to us from the past but also continuing to develop today.

This is not a book primarily for the academic purist – it is for those whose souls yearn for God. While it is clearly absurd to suggest that prayers from fifth-century Ireland are identical to seventeenth-century prayers from the Hebrides or twentieth-century prayers from Northumbria, there are, however, common strands: a profound trinitarianism, a poetic imagery, an ability to recognise the divine in everyday events, a longing for social justice, a concern for the natural world, a willingness to ask God's blessing on friend or stranger, and a rhythmic approach that seems to blend our own heartbeat with that of God. The repetitious style and common images are, in fact, remarkably difficult to forge.

This collection quite deliberately places well-known traditional material alongside modern previously unpublished prayers, for two reasons:

first, to underline the fact that all prayer, from whatever age, is real now. Those Christians who first uttered their prayers centuries ago are now in heaven. As we pray, using their same words, we unite with them across time: we become the Communion of Saints praying to the God who is himself beyond time and eternity.

Secondly, these – and all – prayers are not primarily intended simply for repetitious use. They exist to help us create our own prayers, perhaps in styles similar to those in this book. Indeed, there are prayers here created at the end of the twentieth century, as a direct result of workshops exploring the Celtic spirituality of the past.

If you find these prayers helpful either for personal or corporate use, then that is good. What is even better is to develop your own prayer life, which helps you to relate to the extraordinary God who is ever-present in the ordinary. To do so in a way that is rhythmic, full of imagery and outgoing is thoroughly consistent with our Celtic forebears.

As you do so,
May the eyes of the Creator behold you,
May the hands of the Saviour uphold you,
May the arms of the Spirit enfold you.
Amen.

Martin Wallace

WAKING UP

Morning prayer

Christ be with me, Christ within me,
Christ behind me, Christ before me,
Christ beside me, Christ to win me,
Christ to comfort and restore me,
Christ beneath me, Christ above me,
Christ in quiet, Christ in danger,
Christ in hearts of all that love me,
Christ in mouth of friend and stranger.

St Patrick (5th century)

❋

The Presence

I awake this morning
In the presence
    of the holy angels of God.
May heaven open wide before me
Above me and around me
That I may see
    the Christ of my love
And his sunlit company
In all the things of earth this day.

Iona Community

Arising

I rise up clothed in strength of Christ.
I shall not be imprisoned,
I shall not be harmed;
I shall not be downtrodden,
I shall not be left alone;
I shall not be tainted,
I shall not be overwhelmed.
I go clothed in Christ's white garments;
I go freed to weave Christ's patterns;
I go loved to serve Christ's weak ones;
I go armed to rout out Christ's foes.

Community of Aidan and Hilda

The caim

Circle me Lord
Keep protection near
And danger afar.

Circle me Lord
Keep hope within
Keep doubt without.

Circle me Lord
Keep light near
And darkness afar.

Circle me Lord
Keep peace within
Keep evil out.

David Adam

(Celtic Christians prayed the caim prayers
by extending the forefinger of the right hand
and drawing an imaginary circle around
themselves, asking for protection.)

The night flees

I hear the breeze;
The Spirit moves,
The dark night flees
and God approves;
Christ, God's own Son
takes my confession,
With him I'll run
I'm his possession.

Ramon Beeching

Morning creed

I believe, O God of all gods,
That thou art the eternal Father of life;
I believe, O God of all gods,
That thou art the eternal Father of love.

I believe, O Lord and God of the peoples,
That thou art the creator of the high heavens,
That thou art the creator of the skies above,
That thou art the creator of the oceans below.

I believe, O Lord and God of the peoples,
That thou art He who created my soul
  and set its warp.
Who created my body from dust
  and from ashes,
Who gave to my body breath
  and to my soul its possession.

Father, bless to me my body,
Father, bless to me my soul,
Father, bless to me my life,
Father, bless to me my belief.

Carmina Gadelica
(19th century collection from the Hebrides)

Morning desires

All that I am I give to you Lord
All that I am I give you.

All that I have I share with you Lord
All that I have I share with you.

All my life is yours Lord
All my life is yours.

All my desires are yours Lord
All my desires are yours.

All my hopes are in you Lord
All my hopes are in you.

All I want is you Lord
All I want is you.

David Adam

Enfolding

God to enfold me,
    God to surround me,
God in my speaking,
    God in my thinking.

God in my sleeping,
    God in my waking,
God in my watching,
    God in my hoping.

God in my life,
    God in my lips,
God in my soul,
    God in my heart.

Carmina Gadelica

STARTING THE DAY

Adoration

I bow before the Father
Who made me.
I bow before the Son
Who saved me.
I bow before the Spirit
Who guides me.
In love and adoration
I give my lips
I give my heart
I give my strength.
I bow and adore thee
Sacred Three
The Ever One
The Trinity.

David Adam

Morning praise

May the saints and angels be with me
From the top of my head
To the soles of my feet.

In the company of your saints
I would live this day;
As they lived their lives for you
So may I live this day.

With them to you I bring
My morning praise;
Heavenly chorus I would echo
In my morning praise.

Where they for ever dwell
There would I be;
In heaven to live with you
There may I be.

Mary Calvert

Washing

The three palmfuls of the Sacred Three
To preserve you from every envy, evil eye
    and death;
The palmful of the God of life;
The palmful of the God of love;
The palmful of the Spirit of peace,
Trinity of grace.

Carmina Gadelica (adapted)

May this water be for your healing
In the holy name of the Father,
In the holy name of the Son,
In the holy name of the Spirit,
In the holy name of the Three,
Everlasting, kindly, wise.

Carmina Gadelica (adapted)

The Cross

May the cross of Christ be over this face
    and this ear;
May the cross of Christ be over this mouth
    and this throat;
May the cross of Christ be over my arms
From my shoulders to my hands.

May the cross of Christ be with me,
    before me;
May the cross of Christ be with me,
    behind me.

With the cross of Christ may I meet every
difficulty in the heights and in the depths.

From the top of my head to the nail
    of my foot
I trust in the protection of your Cross,
    O Christ.

From verses attributed to Mugron
(Abbot of Iona, from 965)

Flowing free

The love of God
Flowing free
The love of God
Flow out through me.

The peace of God
Flowing free
The peace of God
Flow out through me.

The life of God
Flowing free
The life of God
Flow out through me.

David Adam

This day

Come I this day to the Father,
Come I this day to the Son,
Come I to the Holy Spirit powerful;
Come I this day with God,
Come I this day with Christ,
Come I with the Spirit of kindly balm.

God, and Spirit, and Jesus,
From the crown of my head
To the soles of my feet;
Come I with my reputation,
Come I with my testimony,
Come I to Thee, Jesu;
    Jesu, shelter me.

Carmina Gadelica

The new creation

As I put on the Belt of Truth, may your
Spirit this day lead me into all truth.

As I put on the Breastplate of Righteousness,
may my washing in the waters of baptism
make me clean from all sin.

As I put on the Helmet of Salvation, may I
be transformed by the renewing of my mind.

As I take up the Shield of Faith, may my
faith in what you have wrought in me
never waver.

As I put on the shoes of the preparation
of the Gospel of Peace, may I be alert
to make known the workings of the Father
through the Son.

As I take up the Sword of the Spirit,
may the renewing power of your word
prevail in my life this day.

Michael Halliwell

Fully dressed

Lord, clothe me with Compassion;
 a sorrow for each other's needs.
Lord, clothe me with Kindness;
 a willingness to serve.
Lord, clothe me with Humility;
 an attitude of mind.
Lord, clothe me with Gentleness;
 the way of Christ in me.
Lord, clothe me with Patience;
 to accept and understand.

Lord, help me to forgive.
 Forgive, Lord, as you've forgiven me.

It seems Lord I am fully dressed;
 yet you say, I'm naked still.

Over all these garments, Lord,
Clothe me with your Love
And Peace within your Will.

Ruth Newman (based on Colossians 3.12-15)

MOVING AROUND

For God's safe keeping

May the strength of God pilot us.
May the power of God preserve us.
May the wisdom of God instruct us.
May the hand of God protect us.
May the way of God direct us.
May the shield of God defend us.
May the host of God guard us
Against the snares of the evil one
And the temptations of the world.
May Christ be with us
Christ above us
Christ in us
Christ before us.
May thy salvation O Lord,
Be always ours
This day and for evermore.
Amen.

St Patrick (5th century)

Day by day

Early in the morning I wait on you,
    O Lord;
Day by day I toil for you,
    O Lord;
At the bright noonday I recollect you,
    O Lord;
In talk and recreation I enjoy you,
    O Lord;
In study and in prayer I learn of you,
    O Lord;
At nightfall and in deep sleep I rest in you,
    O Lord.

Ray Simpson

Walking

I walk in the joy of the Creator.
I walk in the love of the Son.
I walk in the power of the Spirit.
God the Creator, bless my eyes as they see,
God the Son, be ever close to me,
God the Spirit, protect and guide me.
Amen.

Daphne Bridges

The journey

Bless to me, O God,
The earth beneath my foot,
Bless to me, O God,
The path whereon I go;
Bless to me, O God,
The thing of my desire;
Thou Evermore of evermore,
Bless thou to me my rest.

Bless to me the thing
Whereon is set my mind,
Bless to me the thing
Whereon is set my love;
Bless to me the thing
Whereon is set my hope;
O thou King of kings,
Bless thou to me mine eye!

Carmina Gadelica

Each road

May God make safe to you each steep,
May God make open to you each pass,
May God make clear to you each road,
And may he take you in the clasp
  of his own two hands.

Carmina Gadelica

Pentecost

Flame of purity:	Light us up
Flame of beauty:	Light us up
Flame of wisdom:	Light us up
Flame of friendship:	Light us up
Flame of true speech:	Light us up
Flame of true seeing:	Light us up
Flame of winging:	Light us up
Flame of kindling:	Light us up

Community of Aidan and Hilda

Iona: the pilgrim way

I lift my eyes to the mountain,
I trace the long finger of sea,
I set my face to the island
From whence comes a yearning to be
Caught to the margins of Christendom
Where justice and peace form a core
Of love for God's earth
    and one's neighbour
And a longing to take to the poor
The good news
    that will conquer oppression,
That will set the imprisoned free
By the power of the Spirit ne'er ending
Who invites all, partake, even me!
Yes! e'en me who can walk past a beggar
Or fail to be moved by the plight
Of the war-worn, the famished, the dying,
Or the refugee, forced into flight.
But if I wish to cast off this bondage
Which power, wealth and comfort induce
By the grace of the heaven-sent Spirit
This small island might help me
    break loose.

Trevor Thorn

We are filled

Spirit of God
The breath of creation is yours.

Spirit of God
The groans of the world are yours.

Spirit of God
The wonder of communion is yours.

Spirit of God
The fire of love is yours.

And we are filled
And we are filled.

Community of Aidan and Hilda

Alone I stand

Where the sky meets the land
And the sea turns dark,
There I stand, alone and stark.

Where the sky meets the sea
And the land turns green,
There I stand, man and God between.

Where the land meets the sea
And the sky turns blue,
There I stand alone and true.

Alone I stand midst God and man,
Alone I stand midst sky and sand.

I stand as the door through which
    men pass,
As the door where the knocking
    is heard at last.

Laurie Main

❋

BEING WITH OTHERS

Little Trinities

Three things are pleasant in a home:
Good food upon the table;
A man who lovingly kisses his wife;
Children who refrain from quarrelling.

Three attitudes are godly in the Church:
True love of the Lord himself;
Kindness amongst the pews;
A fair dealing with self.

Three ideas enlarge a man's mind:
A humble heart;
A generous soul;
Honesty in businesses.

Three things I wish for myself:
True spiritual beauty;
A heart of giving;
*Grey eyes with pools of true meaning.

Janet Donaldson
*(*Adapt the colour to your own choice!)*

The heavenly banquet

I would like to have the men of heaven
In my own house:
With vats of good cheer
Laid out for them.

I would like to have all the saints,
Their fame is so great.
I would like people
From every corner of heaven.

I would like them to be cheerful
In their drinking.
I would like to have Jesus too
Here amongst them.

I would like a great lake of beer
For the King of Kings,
I would like to be watching heaven's family
Drinking it through all eternity.

Source unknown (10th century)

Christmas poor

You are the caller
You are the poor
You are the stranger at my door.

You are the wanderer
The unfed
You are the homeless
With no bed.

You are the man
Driven insane
You are the child
Crying in pain.

You are the other who comes to me
If I open to another you're born in me.

David Adam

Reminder of your love

Thank you for our legs,
As we pilgrimage through life,
Thank you for our hands,
As we wield bread and knife,
Thank you for our bodies,
As we see our children grow,
Thank you for our faces,
In them the Christ we know,
Thank you for our eyes
As we wonder at creation,
Thank you for our hearts
As we accept your salvation.
Amen.

Anne Smith

Peace

Peace between neighbours,
Peace between kindred,
Peace between lovers,
In love of the King of life.

Peace between person and person,
Peace between wife and husband,
Peace between woman and children,
The peace of Christ above all peace.

Bless, O Christ, my face,
Let my face bless every thing;
Bless, O Christ, mine eye,
Let mine eye bless all it sees.

Carmina Gadelica

Shabbat

Bless, O Lord,
    this food we are about to eat,
    and we pray you, O God
that it may be good
    for our body and soul,
and if there is any poor creature
    hungry or thirsty walking the road
may God send him in to us
    so that we can share the food
    with him,
just as Christ shares his gifts
    with all of us.
Amen.

Northumbrian Office

*

Wedding song

Father, give your love
And build it in us your servants,
Guide us to share love every day;
Create in each an affection
Reflecting your love,
Generous beyond the world's way.

Jesus, give your peace
And grow it in us your servants,
Hold it in our homes every day;
May it flow outwards
To those we encounter
As witness that peace is your way.

Spirit, give your joy
And spread it through us your servants,
Help us be joyful every day;
With love and peace, may
Our joy be in great abundance
As we build life in your way.

Trevor Thorn
(written for a step-daughter's wedding)

Fa - ther, give your love And build it in us your ser - vants, Guide us to share love ev - ery day; Cre - ate in each an a - ffec - tion Re - flec - ting your love, Gen' - rous be - yond the world's way.

ON ACTIVE SERVICE

Bless each thing

Bless to me, O God,
  Each thing mine eye sees;
Bless to me, O God,
  Each sound mine ear hears;
Bless to me, O God,
  Each odour that goes to my nostrils;
Bless to me, O God,
    Each taste that goes to my lips;
    Each note that goes to my song,
    Each ray that guides my way,
    Each thing that I pursue,
    Each lure that tempts my will,
    The zeal that seeks my living soul,
The Three that seek my heart,
    The zeal that seeks my living soul,
The Three that seek my heart.

Carmina Gadelica

No shelter

Lord,
   Let our memory
   provide no shelter
   for grievance against another.

Lord,
   Let our heart
   provide no harbour
   for hatred of another.

Lord,
   Let our tongue
   be no accomplice
   in the judgement of a brother.

Northumbrian Office

Mary's Son

Mary's Son, my friend,
Come and bless the kitchen.
May we have fullness through you.

Mary's Son, my friend,
Come and bless the school.
May we have fullness through you.

Mary's Son, my friend,
Come and bless the soil.
May we have fullness through you.

Mary's Son, my friend,
Come and bless the work.
May we have fullness through you.

Mary's Son, my friend,
Come and bless the church.
May we have fullness through you.

Community of Aidan and Hilda

Milking

Bless, O God, my little cow,
  Bless, O God, my desire;
Bless thou my partnership
  And the milking of my hands, O God.

Bless, O God, each teat,
  Bless, O God, each finger;
Bless thou each drop
  That goes into my pitcher, O God!

Carmina Gadelica

The warrior

In the strength of the Warrior of God,
I oppose all that pollutes;
In the eye of the Face of God,
I expose all that deceives;
In the energy of the Servant of God,
I bind up all that is broken.

Ray Simpson

My plants

In the morning, my Lord, I offer you praise
As I water my plants set out in their trays,
As I think of the roots,
    to make the plant strong,
And I feed on your Word,
    which never is wrong,
As I look at the leaves,
    turned face to the sun,
May I look towards you
    until this day is done,
As I admire the bright flowers,
Giving glory to you,
May I bring you pleasure
    in the things that I do,
As I look at the fruit, tasty and sweet,
May I taste of you to the people I meet,
As I think of the seed, hidden away,
May I plant one seed for you on this day,
In the morning, my Lord, I offer you praise
As I water my plants set out in their trays.

Craig Roberts

A painful chest

Power of heaven have I over you;
Power of universe have I over you;
Power of sun have I over you;
Power of earth have I over you;
Power of saints have I over you;
Power of God have I over you.

Carmina Gadelica (adapted)

Pruning shrubs

God the creator, renew this plant's growth.
Christ the carpenter, bless the use
    of this tool.
Spirit who guides, control my hand's work.
    Father of life, bless your good earth.
    Son who redeems, give gardens
    new birth.
    Spirit enlightening, show us their worth.
    Amen.

Daphne Bridges

Creation

There is no plant in the ground
But tells of your beauty, O Christ.
There is no creature on the earth
There is no life in the sea
But proclaims your goodness.
There is no bird on the wing
There is no star in the sky
There is nothing beneath the sun
But is full of your blessing.
Lighten my understanding
Of your presence all around, O Christ.
Kindle my will
     to be caring for Creation.

Iona Community

RESTING

At evening time

Come, Lord Jesus,
You too were tired
When day was done;
You met your friends
at evening time.
COME, LORD JESUS.

Come, Lord Jesus,
You too enjoyed
When nights drew on;
You told your tales at close of day.
COME, LORD JESUS.

Come, Lord Jesus.
You kindled faith
When lamps were low;
You opened scriptures,
broke the bread
and shed your light
As darkness fell.
COME, LORD JESUS, MEET US HERE.

Iona Community

Day end

Let the day end,
the night fall,
the world move into silence,
And let God's people say Amen.
AMEN.

Let minds unwind,
hearts be still,
bodies relax,
And let God's people say Amen.
AMEN.

But before the day is done,
Let God's holy name be praised,
And let God's people say Amen.
AMEN.

Iona Community

Silence

I weave a silence on to my lips
I weave a silence into my mind
I weave a silence within my heart.
I close my ears to distractions
I close my eyes to attractions
I close my heart to temptations.

David Adam

Healing waters

Lord, immerse us in the ocean of your love.
Bathe us in your cleansing rivers.
Soak us in your healing waters.
Drench us in your powerful downfalls.
Cool us in your bracing baths.
Refresh us in your sparkling streams.
Master us in your mighty seas.
Calm us by your quiet pools.

Community of Aidan and Hilda

Heavenly balm

Quieten me, quieten me, O Lord:
ease me from the intense busy-ness
   that assails me.

Quieten me, quieten me, O Lord:
draw me away from the incessant noise.

Still me, still me, O God:
Help me to yield up the need to chatter.

Still me, still me, O God:
Let me be immersed in your deep stillness.

Then, Lord,
When my heart, my soul, my mind
   and my spirit are at rest,
Open me to hear your voice of calm.

And, Lord,
In that deep stillness of eternity,
Bestow on me your heavenly balm.

Trevor Thorn

Never-failing love

Still me, calm me,
Like the peace of a mountain lake
    on a gentle sunny day.

Cleanse me, release me,
Like the stormy winds which blow away
    the early morning mist.

Kindle me, renew me,
With the flickering flames of your Spirit.

Hold me, touch me,
Like a mother with a child at her breast.

Enfold me, sustain me,
With your never-failing love.

Caroline Baston

✳

The Holy Trinity

(set to the music of *The Iona Boat Song*)

To the Trinity Three
Now bend we the knee,
To the one who is love evermore.
And we come to the throne
Of our God, Three in One,
Whose glory we praise and adore.

O Creator of all
Low before you we fall
As we give you thanksgiving and praise.
Blessed Jesus, the Son,
Of our God, Three in One,
Be our Guide to the end of our days.

Holy Spirit of grace
Be with us in this place
And grant us your gifts from above.
Gracious Spirit of power
Fill our lives at this hour
And pour out on us blessings and love.
To the Trinity Three

Now bend we the knee,
To the One who is Love evermore,
And we come to the throne
Of our God, Three in One,
Whose glory we praise and adore.

Derrick Cooling

Resting blessing

In name of the Lord Jesus,
And of the Spirit of healing balm,
In name of the Father of Israel,
     I lay me down to rest.

If there be evil threat or quirk,
Or covert act intent on me,
God free me and encompass me,
     And drive from me mine enemy.

In name of the Father precious,
And of the Spirit of healing balm,
In name of the Lord Jesus,
     I lay me down to rest.

God, help me and encompass me,
From this hour till the hour of my death.

Carmina Gadelica

*

SLEEPING

Closing prayer

I lie down this night with God
And God will lie down with me.
I lie down this night with Christ
And Christ will lie down with me.
I lie down this night with the Spirit
And the Spirit will lie down with me.
The Three of my love
    will be lying down with me.
I shall not lie down with sin
Nor shall sin or sin's shadow
    lie down with me.
I lie down this night with God
And God will lie down with me.

Iona Community

Night prayer

As I lay down to sleep,
May the holiness of the Trinity
In love enfold me.
With power protect me.

May the Father who creates,
    surround me,
The Son who redeems,
    restore me,
The Spirit who enlightens,
    bring peace.

May angels watch over me
Within these walls
In the silence of the night.

Bronwen Vizard

This night

May God bless us
In our sleep with rest,
In our dreams with vision,
In our waking with a calm mind,
In our souls with the friendship of
the Holy Spirit
This night and every night.
Amen.

Iona Community

Protection

May God shield me,
May God fill me,
May God keep me,
May God watch me.

May God bring me
      To the land of peace
      To the country of the King,
To the peace of eternity.

Carmina Gadelica

Brigid: night office

I make Christ's Cross over my face
I make Christ's Cross over my eyes

[In small groups each person may make the
sign of the Cross and say these words in turn]

Each day and each night
that I place myself under their keeping:

I shall not be forgotten
I shall not be destroyed
I shall not be imprisoned
I shall not be harassed by evil powers.

Nightmares shall not lie on me
Black thoughts shall not lie on me
Bad images shall not lie on me
No ill-will of enemy shall lie on me.

Community of Aidan and Hilda

Simplicity

May the blessing of the Son
help you do what must be done,

May the Spirit stroke your brow
as weary down to sleep you go,

May the Father mark your rest
empower you for tomorrow's test,

May the trinity rekindle
the pure flames of your life's candle.

Ramon Beeching

Lying down

God with me lying down,
God with me rising up,
God with me in each ray of light,
Nor I a ray of joy without him,
　　Nor one ray without him.

Christ with me sleeping,
Christ with me waking,
Christ with me watching,
Every day and night,
　　Each day and night.

God with me protecting,
The Lord with me directing,
The Spirit with me strengthening,
For ever and for evermore,
　　Ever and evermore, Amen.
　　　Chief of chiefs, Amen.

Carmina Gadelica

Grannie's prayer for Iona

May your nights be blessed
With peaceful sleep
And angels guard your bed.

May your days be blessed
With contentment,
From the flowing milk you're fed.

May stars shine
Through your window,
And the white moon smile on you.

And in the daylight hours
God's sun beam at you too.

Amen.

Margaret Wallis

Final journey

Going home

I am going home with You, to your home,
    to your home;
I am going home with You,
    to your home of mercy
I am going home with You, to your home,
    to your home;
I am going home with You,
    to the Fount of all the blessings.

Carmina Gadelica (adapted)

Sunset

Lord of the sunset,
As I go to my eternal home,
Strengthen me on my last journey with you
That I may entrust my soul into your hands
In faith and hope.

Michael Halliwell

Dying

In the name of the all powerful Father,
In the name of the all loving Son,
In the name of the all pervading Spirit.
I command all spirit of fear to leave you,
I break the power of unforgiven sin in you,
I set you free from dependence
    upon human ties
That you may be as free as the wind,
As soft as sheep's wool,
As straight as an arrow;
And that you may journey
    into the Heart of God.

Community of Aidan and Hilda

Protection

My good angel, messenger of God,
Protect my body and my soul;
Protect me from the evil spirit
And above all else from sin.
I pray you, saints, men and women,
I pray you, Jesus,
To protect me and obtain for me
A good and happy death.

Traditional (from Brittany)

55

Gate

Saviour and Friend, how wonderful art thou,
My companion upon the changeful way,
The comforter of its weariness,
My guide to the Eternal Town,
The welcome at its gate.

Traditional

Eternal home

Go forth upon your journey from this world,
In the Name of God the Father
    who created you;
In the Name of Jesus Christ
    who died for you;
In the Name of the Holy Spirit
    who shines through you;
In friendship with God's saints;
Aided by the holy angels.
May you rest this day
In the peace and love
Of your eternal home.

Traditional (adapted)

BLESSING

Deep peace

Deep peace of the running wave to you
Deep peace of the flowing air to you
Deep peace of the quiet earth to you
Deep peace of the shining stars to you
Deep peace of the Son of peace to you.

Scots Traditional

Father

Father, bless to me my body,
Father, bless to me my soul,
Father, bless to me my life,
Father, bless to me my belief.

Carmina Gadelica

Trinity

God to guard you,
God to guide you,
God to keep you,
God to hide you
In his bosom,
Evermore.

Son to watch you,
Son to teach you,
Son to help you,
Son to heal you
With his life,
His blood outpoured.

Spirit with you,
Spirit in you,
Spirit through you,
Spirit show you
You are God's love,
Evermore.

Laurie Main

Love and affection

The love and affection of the angels
    be to you,
The love and affection of the saints
    be to you,
The love and affection of heaven
    be to you,
To guard you and to cherish you.
May God shield you on every steep,
May Christ aid you on every path,
May Spirit fill you on every slope,
On hill and on plain.

Carmina Gadelica

Guarding

The guarding of the God of life be on you,
The guarding of loving Christ be on you,
The guarding of Holy Spirit be on you
Every night of your lives,
    To aid you and enfold you
    Each day and night of your lives.

Carmina Gadelica

59

Your peace

I am bending my knee
In the eye of the Father who created me,
In the eye of Son who died for me,
In the eye of the Spirit who cleansed me,
    In love and desire.

Pour down upon us from heaven
The rich blessing of thy forgiveness;
Thou who art uppermost in the City,
    Be thou patient with us.

Grant to us, thou Saviour of Glory,
The fear of God,
The love of God,
And his affection,
And the will of God to do on earth
    at all times
As angels and saints do in heaven;
Each day and night give us thy peace.
    Each day and night give us thy peace.

Carmina Gadelica

Pentecost blessing

Deep warmth of joy and love be yours,
Bright light of sight and life be yours,
Rich glow of fruits and growth be yours;
  Fire of the Spirit burn within you
  Fire of the Spirit burn within you

  Energy of God empower you
  Flame of the Spirit anoint you
  Influence of God sustain you.

Breath of God fill you and dwell in you,
Life of God inspire and renew you,
Breeze of God revive and disturb you;
  Wind of the Spirit blow through you
  Wind of the Spirit blow through you.

  Life giving presence of God stir you
  Unseen power of God strengthen you
  Wellspring of truth cleanse you
    and lead you.

The Spirit encourage and guide you,
Creative voice of God direct you
And kindle adventure within you;
    Wild Goose cheer you and call you on
    Wild Goose cheer you and call you on.

Craufurd Murray

Now and evermore

God who made us, we worship you.
Christ who saved us, we thank you.
Spirit who strengthens, we need you.
    God the Father bless our days.
    God the Son we give you praise.
    God the Spirit guide our ways
    Now and evermore.
    Amen.

Daphne Bridges

A Christmas blessing

May the trust of Mary
    troubled by her strange call
And Joseph's encouragement
    beside her through all
Be God's gift to you.

May the radiant brightness
    and light of the Star
The hope and longing of searchers
    travelling from afar
Be God's gift to you.

May the wonder of shepherds
    surprised by God's love
The deep joy of the angels
    who came from above
Be God's gift to you.

May the peace of the Christ-Child
    in carved trough of stone
Sounding the word Saviour
    fashioned by Grace alone
Be God's great gift to you.

Craufurd Murray

These hands

With these hands I bless the lonely,
    the forgotten and the lost;
With these hands I shield you messengers
    from attacks within, without;
With these hands I dispel darkness
    and rebuke evil forces;
With these hands I pray your victory
    for fighting ones and dying.

Community of Aidan and Hilda

Smooring the fire

The sacred Three
To save,
To shield,
To surround
The hearth,
The house,
The household,
This eve,
This night,
Oh! this eve,
This night,
And every night,
Each single night.
                    Amen.

Carmina Gadelica

The house

The Father is in the house
Nothing need we fear

Christ is in the house
Loving us so dear

The Spirit is in the house
Listening to our prayer

The Three are in the house
Always very near

David Adam

My repose

God, bless to me this day,
God, bless to me this night;
Bless, O bless, thou God of grace,
Each day and hour of my life;
    Bless, O bless, thou God of grace,
    Each day and hour of my life.

God, bless the pathway on which I go,
God bless the earth that is beneath
    my sole;
Bless, O God and give to me thy love,
O God of gods, bless my rest
    and my repose;
    Bless, O God, and give to me
    thy love,
    And bless, O God of gods, my repose.

Carmina Gadelica

An Irish blessing

May the road rise to meet you
May the wind be always at your back
May the sun shine warm upon your face
The rain fall soft upon your fields
And until we meet again
May God hold you
In the hollow of his hand.

Traditional

INDEX OF FIRST LINES

INDEX OF AUTHORS
AND SOURCES

ACKNOWLEDGEMENTS

The compiler and publisher gratefully acknowledge permission to reproduce copyright material in this anthology. Every effort has been made to trace owners of copyright material and the compiler apologizes for any inadvertent omissions. Full acknowledgement will be made in future editions.

David Adam, *The Edge of Glory*, SPCK, 1985 (pp. 4, 7, 9, 26, 41, 66); *Tides and Seasons*, SPCK, 1989 (p. 13).

Mary Calvert, *God to Enfold*, Grail, 1993 (p. 10). Ray Simpson, *Resources for Worship in the Celtic Tradition*, The Community of Aidan and Hilda, Redhill Christian Centre, Snitterfield, Stratford-upon-Avon CV39 OPQ (pp. 3, 20, 22, 34, 41, 50, 55, 64).

Ray Simpson, *Exploring Celtic Spirituality*, Hodder and Stoughton, 1995 (pp. 18, 35).

Each Day and Each Night, Wild Goose Publications, 1994, adapted from traditional Scots Gaelic prayers found in *Carmina Gadelica*, collected by Alexander Carmichael, 1900 (pp. 2, 38, 47).

A Northumbrian Office, The Northumbria Community, Nether Springs Trust, Hetton Hall, Chatton, Alnwick NE66 5SD (pp. 29, 33).

A Wee Worship Book, Wild Goose Worship Group, 1989, copyright 1989 WGRG, Iona Community, Glasgow G51 3UU Scotland (pp. 39, 40, 49).